IF FOUND PLE/

GW01458015

👤 _____

✉ _____

📱 _____

Greater Than a Tourist Book Series
Reviews from Readers

GREATER THAN A TOURIST- PERTH WESTERN AUSTRALIA AUSTRALIA

50 Travel Tips from a Local

Nikkita-Leigh Dixon & Cindy Arlott

Cover designed by: Lisa Rusczyk Ed. D.

Cover Image: https://pixabay.com/photos/sea-sand-albany-australia-rocks-2426998/

Editor: Amanda Wills

CZYK
PUBLISHING

CZYK Publishing Since 2011.

Greater Than a Tourist
Visit our website at GreaterThanaTourist.com

Lock Haven, PA
All rights reserved.

ISBN: 9781097193080

>TOURIST

50 TRAVEL TIPS FROM A LOCAL

BOOK DESCRIPTION

Are you excited about planning your next trip?

Do you want to try something new?

Would you like some guidance from a local?

If you answered yes to any of these questions, then this Greater Than a Tourist book is for you.

Greater Than A Tourist - Perth Western Australia, Australia by Nikkita-Leigh Dixon and Cindy Arlott offers the inside scoop on Perth. Most travel books tell you how to travel like a tourist. Although there is nothing wrong with that, as part of the Greater Than a Tourist series, this book will give you travel tips from someone who has lived at your next travel destination.

In these pages, you will discover advice that will help you throughout your stay. This book will not tell you exact addresses or store hours but instead will give you excitement and knowledge from a local that you may not find in other smaller print travel books.

Travel like a local. Slow down, stay in one place, and get to know the people and culture. By the time you finish this book, you will be eager and prepared to travel to your next destination.

Inside this travel guide book you will find:

- Insider tips from a local.

- Packing and planning list.

- List of travel questions to ask yourself or others while traveling.

OUR STORY

Traveling is a passion of the "Greater than a Tourist" series creator. Lisa studied abroad in college, and for their honeymoon Lisa and her husband toured Europe. During her travels to Malta, an older man tried to give her some advice based on his own experience living on the island since he was a young boy. She was not sure if she should talk to the stranger but was interested in his advice. When traveling to some places she was wary to talk to locals because she was afraid that they weren't being genuine. Through her travels, Lisa learned how much locals had to share with tourists. Lisa created the *Greater Than a Tourist* book series to help connect people with locals. A topic that locals are very passionate about sharing.

TABLE OF CONTENTS

15. Enjoy A Flutter At The Casino
16. Take A Step Back In Time At London Court
17. Put On Your Dancing Shoes At 'Connies'
18. Try Perth's Best Bottle Of Red
19. Connect With Nature At Yanchep National Park
20. Spend A Day At The Beach
21. Make A Splash At Elizabeth Quay
22. Get To Know Perth's Sporting Roots
23. Watch A Show At The Perth Arena
24. Get Up Close And Personal With Animals
25. Have A Cup Of Joe At The Cappuccino Strip
26. Peruse The Unique Fremantle Markets
27. Watch The Sun Set Over The City Skyline
28. Get Involved In Perth's Local Music Scene
29. Get Your Culture Fix At The Heath Ledger Theatre
30. See Local Wildlife Up Close At Penguin Island
31. Skydive Onto The Beach
32. See The Bon Scott Memorial
33. Hear The Crashing Of Serpentine Falls
34. Get A Revolving View Of The City
35. Run Away And Join The Circus
36. Work On Your Tan At Cottesloe Beach
37. Get Lost In A Book At The State Library
38. Brush Up On Your History
39. Hear The Bells Ring

Perth
Western Australia, Australia

Perth Climate

	High	Low
January	87	66
February	88	67
March	84	65
April	77	59
May	71	54
June	67	51
July	65	49
August	66	50
September	69	50
October	72	55
November	77	59
December	82	63

GreaterThanaTourist.com

Temperatures are in Fahrenheit degrees.
Source: NOAA

DEDICATION

This book is dedicated to my mum Cindy Arlott who co-wrote this text with me. She has been supportive of my every life decision and followed me from Perth to London and back again so I would always have somewhere close by to call home. Truly the best mum one could hope for!

ABOUT THE AUTHOR

Nikkita Dixon is a journalist and social media manager. She was born in Subiaco in Perth and left at the age of 25 to travel the world. She has a Bachelor of Communications, majoring in Journalism and Broadcast.

These days she spends her days writing articles from various beaches across South East Asia. Nikkita loves to sing, play guitar and is slowly working toward her skydiving license.

Cindy Arlott is Nikkita's mother and the founder of the Absolutely Australia website. She was also born in Perth and has spent the past 20 years working as a web designer and content curator.

Cindy loves spending time in her garden, making organic beauty products and playing with her dog Rocky.

HOW TO USE THIS BOOK

The *Greater Than a Tourist* book series was written by someone who has lived in an area for over three months. The goal of this book is to help travelers either dream or experience different locations by providing opinions from a local. The author has made suggestions based on their own experiences. Please check before traveling to the area in case the suggested places are unavailable.

Travel Advisories: As a first step in planning any trip abroad, check the Travel Advisories for your intended destination.
https://travel.state.gov/content/travel/en/traveladvisories/traveladvisories.html

FROM THE PUBLISHER

Traveling can be one of the most important parts of a person's life. The anticipation and memories that you have are some of the best. As a publisher of the Greater Than a Tourist book series, as well as the popular *50 Things to Know* book series, we strive to help you learn about new places, spark your imagination, and inspire you. Wherever you are and whatever you do I wish you safe, fun, and inspiring travel.

Lisa Rusczyk Ed. D.
CZYK Publishing

WELCOME TO
> TOURIST

Having been born and raised in various parts of Perth and the surrounding suburbs, there isn't much of the city we haven't seen. As the most isolated capital city in the world, Perthians are well known for having holidays in their own backyard – and what better place to do it when we have some of the best natural beauty in the world. Perth is known for its sunny coastline, water sports and the freshest seafood around, as well as the most magnificent camping available.

We love Perth because of its isolation. You would be easily forgiven for thinking it's almost a country unto its own with its unique culture that thrives away from the influences of the other capital cities in Australia.

Perth is also a city that is constantly changing and evolving. Since we moved to the UK three years ago, the dynamics of Perth have continued to grow – one of Australia's best-kept secret!

1. SEE A BEAUTIFUL SUNRISE

There are plenty of beautiful places in Perth to watch the sunrise, but a firm favorite will always be the picturesque Matilda Bay. Head to the popular café, Bayside Kitchen, to sip a frothy cappuccino or hot chocolate while watching the sky change color over the Swan River. Regulars recommend the pancakes with berry compote or poached eggs and smashed avocado, but get there early to avoid the morning rush. If time allows, go for a walk down to the Crawley Edge Boatshed which is the perfect location to take a few vacation photos. The little boat shed's vivid blue paint, set against the vast expanse of water, has been known to create some truly beautiful photographs.

2. FEEL THE BREEZE IN YOUR HAIR ON THE RIVER

Travel up and down the Swan River and explore the wonders of Perth and Fremantle while marvelling at the dramatic Swan River. There are a few cruise operators on the Swan, but the most popular is Captain Cook Cruises which runs trips to Fremantle/Rottnest, as well as wine runs up to the Swan Valley. You can enjoy a relaxed cruise on the Swan River observing its abundant birdlife and relaxing scenery while sampling the region's iconic food and drink. Take in lovely views of the of the Swan River while enjoying a delicious buffet lunch accompanied by local beer and wines. Enjoy this sightseeing experience with a host of inclusions, all for a very reasonable price.

3. DISCOVER THE SECRETS OF SCIENCE

Scitech is a world renowned and multi award-winning not-for-profit organization that operates the Scitech Discovery Centre - a permanent, interactive science museum that includes a planetarium, and is located in West Perth. Scitech features a number of regularly changing, interactive exhibitions designed to inform and educate visitors on subjects concerning science, technology, engineering and math. Offering live science, puppet and planetarium shows presented by enthusiastic science-communications staff. Large feature exhibitions are rotated every six months, but anything on space and astronomy is a real treat. Sit back in their reclining seats and experience the mega 180-degree dome with surround sound and laser projection – a cinematic experience like no other!

4. GET YOUR SPORTS FIX

For those sport enthusiasts on the road (we know there are a lot of you), the Moon Late Night Cafe is likely to end up on your list of stops when you visit Perth. Residents travel up to an hour to watch their teams battle it out in the Premier League, as well as any other sport that might be going at the time. The venue itself is huge, with plenty of nooks for those who like to keep to themselves, plus a giant bar and outdoor area for the lads who fancy making friends or leading the odd football chant.

5. SIP AN ICE-COLD CRAFT BEER

By far the most popular brewery in WA, Little Creatures not only boasts a huge range of craft beers made in house, it is just a really great venue. Set on the waterfront of the Fremantle coastline, Little Creatures has an industrial feel with its open warehouse aesthetic and visible brewing tanks. There are two levels you can find a drinking spot in, including an expansive balcony overlooking the Fremantle docks. The food is delicious whether you choose to drink or not. With wood fire pizza ovens crackling downstairs, it's no secret what their specialty is, but the rest of the menu is classy enough to make Little Creatures the kind of place you'd bring your family to for a nice meal.

6. WATCH THE DOLPHINS PLAY

On the outskirts of Perth is the coastal suburb of Mandurah (although don't go calling it Perth to the locals - until recently it was a city in its own right) which is home to the beautiful Dolphin Quay. This

21

wonderful destination has an array of boutique markets, a man-made beach, a superb park, a lively upmarket tavern and, of course, plenty of dolphins skimming through the water nearby. Top dining recommendations include Punjabi Virsa (I'd challenge you to find a better curry in Perth), Nino's Fish and Chips (with, oddly enough, the biggest *pancakes* you'll ever see, as well as amazing seafood) and the Oyster Bar (for the top live music and fresh-from-the-sea oysters). You can also rent kayaks or a boat from the area if you fancy some water sports on the vast network of canals in Mandurah.

7. TEST YOUR WAKEBOARDING SKILLS

Perth Wake Park is the only cable wakeboard park in Western Australia and is located 30 minutes south of Perth city at the Mundijong Rd, Kwinana Freeway

exit. Riders can enjoy a range of features including a

full-size main cable, a beginner specific cable, a step-

up pool for advanced riders, a café, pro shop and hire

shop. Entry into the park is free for spectators, so

they can sit back and chill on the large veranda

overlooking the main lake and a beach while

watching the activities. Opening hours change with

the seasons and if there are any special events.

8. GET YOUR HEART PUMPING AT ADVENTURE WORLD

Adventure World is Western Australia's only

hybrid theme park/water park. Adventure World

includes world-class attractions such as the Abyss

roller coaster, the Kraken, the longest, tallest and

steepest funnel water slide on the planet, the

23

enchanting Dragon's Kingdom and popular Hawaiian resort-themed Kahuna Falls (an aqua rain fortress) to name a few of the 25 attractions set in beautifully landscaped botanical gardens and lawns. Adventure World is open for seven months a year to take advantage of Western Australia's summer climate. Adventure World is conveniently located adjacent to stunning Bibra Lake , which is a 25 minute drive from the City of Perth and 10 minute drive from the port City of Fremantle.

9. FEED YOUR INNER FOODIE

The Twilight Hawkers Market is in the heart of Perth and is the city's original and biggest street food market with scrumptious food from around the globe. It is held in Forrest Place from 4:30 pm – 9:30 pm every Friday night from October – April each year.

These fantastic markets have made Forrest Place the

place to be on a Friday night for authentic, delicious

street food and live local music . Meet with your

friends after work, grab a pre-show bite or bring the

family into town to enjoy the ambience and

atmosphere of the Twilight Hawkers Market.

10. SEE A LIVE GOLD POUR

Located in Perth, and still operating in the original

heritage premises in the east end of the city, the Perth

Mint is home to the largest coin in the world,

weighing in at one ton of pure gold. The Perth Mint,

Western Australia, manufactures and distributes

platinum, silver and gold coins for collectors and

customers worldwide. The Perth Mint shop is an

authorized stockist of popular brands, including

Argyle Pink Diamonds, Ellendale Yellow Diamonds,

25

Kailis Australian Pearls, Coin Watch timepieces, Pandora Jewelry, Pierre Cardin watches, Guess Jewelry, Waterford, Wedgwood, Royal Selangor, Truffle Hill, Thurlby and many others. Book a tour of their grand heritage building, secured vaults and 1899 melting house where you can see a live gold pour. Afterward, enjoy a guided heritage walk and entrance to the Gold Exhibition.

"Travelling: it leaves you speechless, then turns you into a storyteller."

11. GET YOUR HIKING BOOTS ON

John Forrest National Park was established in 1900, after the state's first premier Sir John Forrest, who was Premier of Western Australia between 1890 and 1901. Located in the Darling Scarp, 24 km east of Perth City, John Forrest National Park is the first national park in Western Australia and the second in Australia, after the Royal National Park. The visitor area contains barbecue and picnic facilities and cultivated gardens of native plants. Several trails run through various parts of the park, including the Railway Heritage Trail, which follows the alignment of the old railway line to York. Visitors can walk through the only historical railway tunnel in WA – the Swan View Tunnel. The Eagle View Walk Trail is a 15 km bushwalking circuit that leads to some of the park's less explored areas.

12. VIEW SOME ARTISTIC MASTERPIECES

The Art Gallery of Western Australia is a public

state art gallery that is part of the Perth Cultural

Centre, in Perth. Established in 1891 in the Old Perth

Gaol, it was known as the Geological Museum and

consisted of geological collections. In 1892,

ethnological and biological exhibits were added, and

in 1897, the museum officially became the Western

Australian Museum and Art Gallery. The current

gallery main building opened in 1979 and will

celebrate its 40th anniversary in 2019. This is linked

to the old court house (The Centenary Galleries)

which house the historical collection. It houses the

state's art collection consisting of over 17,000 works

of art, including around 3,000 Indigenous works.

Ongoing exhibitions include Indigenous traditional

and contemporary art from the Northern Territory and Western Australia, and WA art from the 1820s to 1960s, alongside topical displays on key themes drawn from the collection.

13. TASTE AN AWARD-WINNING SAUSAGE ROLL

Truck stop favourite and multi-award winner at Perth's Royal Show, the Miami Bakehouse has been setting tastebuds alight for years. Having recently branched out as a franchise, the original in the southern suburb of Miami is still the favorite for anyone making the journey to the South West. The modest bakery is open daily with a fully stocked display of cakes, donuts, pies and sausage rolls. Everything is good (as you'll see by the many awards littering the walls), but personal recommendations include the beef, cheese and bacon sausage roll, the vanilla slice and the angel cake for melt-in-your-mouth goodness.

14. TAKE A SELFIE WITH THE HAPPIEST ANIMAL ON EARTH

Rottnest Island sits just offshore from the city of Perth and is a protected nature reserve and home to the quokka - a small wallaby-like marsupial. A quick look at the hashtag #quokkaselfie on Instagram and you will see why this animal has been given title on "Happiest animal on Earth". Rottnest Island is surrounded by white sand beaches and secluded coves, making it a popular holiday spot for people who like fishing, surfing, swimming, boating, diving, snorkeling, bike riding, hiking or just lazing around on the beach enjoying the ambience that is Rottnest.

Rottnest has restaurants and fast food outlets, entertainment venues and interesting drinking establishments. The island has accommodations for those on a budget to those who prefer top luxury, but make sure you book early during the busy season. You can travel arrive by means of your own boat, fly, or relax on one of the Rottnest ferries that travel back and forward regularly during the day from Perth, Fremantle or Hillarys Marina. There are very few vehicles on the island as most visitors walk or ride a bike.

15. ENJOY A FLUTTER AT THE CASINO

A night at the Crown Perth is usually reserved for special occasions for locals, so expect to dress to the nines. The Crown Casino has a huge floor space set alight by dozens of colorful slot machines, poker tables, giant sports TV screens and other games to excite the most astute gambler. At the Crown you can enjoy a flutter on the gaming tables or try your hand at an old Australian pastime known as 'two-up'. Crown Perth has top quality theatre and performance venues which are home to highly acclaimed musicians, sporting events and theatre productions year round. Extraordinary views of Perth's cityscape and the Swan River can be seen from most places around Crown Perth. Whether you are after luxury or affordable accommodations, you will find it at either of the two major hotels in the heart of the complex.

16. TAKE A STEP BACK IN TIME AT LONDON COURT

It is worth going to London Court to see what Perthians think London might be like. It's sort of got that 'ye old England' vibe with dilapidated houses and shop fronts with the odd street lantern, but the shops themselves are an eclectic mix of niche jewelry shops, cafes and the types of places selling kangaroo fur-trimmed notepads. Find London Court down a small lane on the Hay Street Mall in the city centre. With a not very big arcade for fun and entertainment it is worth a little wander through, especially if you're an expat longing for a little bit of home.

17. PUT ON YOUR DANCING SHOES AT 'CONNIES'

One of a small handful of LGBT-friendly destinations in Perth, Connections or 'Connies' is a lively and stylish nightspot with an ever changing dance floor design. Entertaining Perth's gay community since 1975, Connections is separated into three areas - the main dance floor, a relaxed downstairs lounge and an outside terrace. Be prepared for fun-filled debauchery any night of the week, with international DJs, go-go dancers and drag queen shows. Make sure to check out their event listing for familiar faces from Rupaul's Drag Race and the ever popular Lesbian Mud Wrestling.

18. TRY PERTH'S BEST BOTTLE OF RED

Australia is famous for its wine, and Western Australia is high on the list for producing a quality variety of wine. Get yourself a designated driver and plan a wine tasting run to any of the many vineyards surrounding Perth then take home some exceptional wine with you. Take a day trip to the Swan Valley from Perth City to experience the wine, food, and other treats of regional Western Australia as well as the picturesque vineyards. You can explore the Swan Valley on a full-day or half-day trip from Perth. Take a scenic drive to the Bickley Valley and explore more wineries located in the Perth Hills, including Perth's only urban whiskey distillery, with whiskey tastings included. After you have had your fill of Bickley Valley wine, cider, whiskey and food, make time for

35

a picnic or a stop in a quiet spot in this picturesque area which boasts stunning views of rolling hills covered in orchards and plentiful vineyards.

19. CONNECT WITH NATURE AT YANCHEP NATIONAL PARK

This beautiful national park is 50 km north of Perth and its bushland and wetland is home to koalas, western grey kangaroos and rich birdlife. Crystal Cave is an underground limestone cavern with stalactites and stalagmites, though it is only one of many caves in the park. Yanchep National Park is a popular place for a picnic or using one of the many free barbecues overlooking the lake or nestled in the tuart and banksia woodlands. Stroll along the boardwalk and view one of Australia's favourite native animals, the koalas. Early and late in the day you will notice many kangaroos as they come out after spending the day sheltering from the sun under bushes and trees. More than 400 caves have been recorded in the park with many opened for visits. You can also learn the rich culture and history of the Noongar people of Australia's South West.

20. SPEND A DAY AT THE BEACH

Scarborough is one of the many world-class beaches in Perth and is known as a surf hotspot. Scarborough Beach has gone through many transformations over the years, but has always held a special spot in people's hearts as the prime location for hitting the beach or having a summer's evening meal near the beach. Scarborough Beach is a popular surfing beach, with great waves most of the year.

This has also become a very popular windsurfing location. Up and down the coastline you will see the highly visible, landmark high-rise hotel, the Rendezvous Observation City, originally built in Scarborough in 1986. In Scarborough, you will find accommodation, business facilities or a quiet place to drink, have a nice meal, and enjoy some music paired with the fun of a nightlife. If you stay in the hotel you will see the coastline extends for kilometres north and south of you. On a clear day you can see Rottnest and on most evenings you can enjoy beautiful sunsets over the Indian Ocean.

"It's better to see something once than to hear about it a thousand times."

21. MAKE A SPLASH AT ELIZABETH QUAY

Elizabeth Quay is named in honour of Queen Elizabeth I and is a mixed-use development project located where Perth's city meets the Swan River. Elizabeth Quay is the perfect place to relax, dine and play when in Perth City. Elizabeth Quay created new recreational opportunities for Perth locals and visitors alike. Take a walk over the striking bridge to the island's marine-inspired playground, check out the landmark Spanda artwork or grab a quick bite after work. The BHP Water Park is the primary entry point to Elizabeth Quay, it's water feature uses jets, misting, sound and lighting to create an exciting and changeable water choreography that will excite the senses. Families can dig, splash and play around on the nautical-inspired natural playground. The park

39

has a sand pit and log steppers, as well as lots of climbing ropes and frames to scale, a ship's bell to ring and a slide. The Landing is the open space for Elizabeth Quay, hosting a range of lunchtime sporting events, concerts and pop up vendors. You can also stroll around the continuous one-kilometre walkable circuit around the inlet and island. The eastern promenade offers short stay public moorings for those visiting the Quay by boat. Finding something to do and something to see at the Quay is simple.

22. GET TO KNOW PERTH'S SPORTING ROOTS

The WACA has been Western Australia's "home of cricket" since the early 1890s and is the home venue of WA's first-class cricket teams, the Western Warriors and the Western Fury. The Perth Scorchers, a Big Bash League franchise, also play at the ground, which is branded #TheFurnace for those matches. The pitch at the WACA is regarded as one of the quickest and bounciest in the world. The WACA Museum (located on-site) features exhibits about Western Australian cricket. Beginning in the summer of 2018/19 the WACA Ground will cease to serve as the main international cricket venue in Perth. A new 60,000 seat stadium is being constructed in Burswood that will host limited overs internationals, test matches against high-drawing opponents (England, India and South Africa), and domestic Big Bash League (BBL) matches for Perth Scorchers. The WACA Ground will continue to host tests against lower-drawing opponents, Sheffield Shield matches, and will be redeveloped into the state's leading cricket training facility.

23. WATCH A SHOW AT THE PERTH ARENA

Also nicknamed the 'Transformer', this entertainment and sporting arena is nestled right in the city centre of Perth and used mostly for basketball matches and concerts. The 15,000-capacity arena features a breathtaking design and world-leading technology. The Perth Arena is located on Wellington Street near the site of the former Perth Entertainment Centre. The venue has a retractable roof, 36 luxury appointed corporate suites, a 680-bay underground car park and five dedicated function spaces. The Perth Arena is the busiest venue in Western Australia, with many local, regional and international artists having staged their performances at the arena.

24. GET UP CLOSE AND PERSONAL WITH ANIMALS

The Perth Zoo is a pleasant ferry trip across the Swan River from Perth City. Over twelve decades, the Perth Zoo has grown from a place of recreation and fascination to one of education, conservation and inspiration. Playgrounds, barbecues, mechanised rides, animal encounters and a packed season of events still delight thousands of families every year. Now the Perth Zoo shows animals in appropriate social groups within naturalistic settings with a priority on their welfare. The zoo has evolved from the cement cages, bars and mesh barriers of yesteryear, after tearing down the elephants' concrete jungle and moving the orangutans out of boxy cages.

Now they offer open exhibits, giving the elephants something closer to the real thing and by building an extensive and dramatic African habitat. The zoo has built towering tree-like structures to get orangutans back up into the vertical sphere closer to their own habitat. Instead of having bars between you and the animals, there are subtler safety barriers such as moats, water bodies and glass. A fun day for the family or to enjoy alone.

25. HAVE A CUP OF JOE AT THE CAPPUCCINO STRIP

Fremantle's South Terrace, otherwise known as the 'Cappuccino Strip', is a bustling mix of cafes, restaurants and pubs. Here you'll notice Fremantle's fascination with all things Italian, boasting some of the best coffee in the state, as well as some truly great pizza and pasta. With a buzzing atmosphere and choices galore, you'll find numerous locally-made, designer clothing shops, gift stores and bookstores. An ideal Sunday afternoon would include a milkshake and a plate of churros from San Churros, either enjoyed on the terrace or inside, on one of their cozy armchairs. After that, have a wander through the corridors of Elizabeth's Second Hand Book Shop where you will find well-loved paperbacks of all genres. Then maybe grab a plate of gourmet pub grub and watch the world go by at the heritage-listed Sail & Anchor Hotel.

26. PERUSE THE UNIQUE FREMANTLE MARKETS

South Terrace is also home to the famous Fremantle Markets - a vibrant hub of eclectic crafts and fresh produce. These markets have been a draw for locals for over a hundred years. More often than not, you'll stop and watch a local performer at the entrance before meandering through the winding walkways filled with a variety of bric-a-bracs and food shacks. Stall holders will usually give you a sample of their wares if you ask nicely.

27. WATCH THE SUN SET OVER THE CITY SKYLINE

A stretch of green space borders the Swan River and is the perfect place to get a good snap of Perth's city skyline. On a still day you can even get a mirror image reflected in the river below. This is the ideal spot to enjoy your fish and chips while you watch Perthians jogging along the pathway with the city humming along across the water. This is another popular vantage point for events like the Australia

Day Skyworks or New Year's Eve fireworks. There's

nothing quite like seeing fireworks from above and

below as you see the display reflected in the water.

28. GET INVOLVED IN PERTH'S LOCAL MUSIC SCENE

One of Perth's more exciting live music venues,

Amplifier, always seems to be one step ahead of the

curve with bands you don't know yet, but will wish

you had in the near future. With an uncanny knack for

searching out live acts that will go the distance,

Amplifier is a hotspot for locals on a Friday or

Saturday night. This holds especially true since the

doors dividing it and neighboring Capitol Nightclub

open at midnight so punters can keep the party going

all night long. Expect there to be a line if you don't

get there early - Amplifier is no secret to Perthians, so it can get a little crowded.

29. GET YOUR CULTURE FIX AT THE HEATH LEDGER THEATRE

There aren't many celebrities Western Australia can claim roots for and one of them, sadly lost in 2008, is now remembered by one of the most beautiful theatre venues in the state. More formally known as the State Theatre Centre of Western Australia, this theatre complex's design was the result of an international design competition in 2005. Gold gilded and visually stunning, the Heath Ledger Theatre plays host to a variety of performing arts events throughout the year.

30. SEE LOCAL WILDLIFE UP CLOSE AT PENGUIN ISLAND

You'll need to book a raft across to this island and pack your own lunch, but it's well worth the effort to see Australia's wildlife in action at this beautiful little island. Penguin Island is home to an array of pelicans, cormorants, pigeons, dolphins, sea lions and, of course, penguins. The island is a great destination for swimming and snorkeling, but most people go for the Discovery Centre where you can get unrestricted underwater views of fairy penguins at play. The Centre has daily commentary and feedings, as well as information panels and touch-tables to help you learn more about the island's inhabitants and history.

"No one realizes how beautiful it is to travel

until he comes home and rests his head

on his old, familiar pillow."

31. SKYDIVE ONTO THE BEACH

Get your adrenaline pumping by strapping yourself in for a tandem skydive right onto the beautiful beaches of Rockingham, a 30-minute drive south of Perth. Jumping at an altitude of 12,000 feet, you'll experience 40 seconds of freefall as you cast your eyes over Perth's stunning coastline. When the moment comes, your parachute will balloon above you, allowing you a peaceful descent right onto the sand.

32. SEE THE BON SCOTT MEMORIAL

As we mentioned earlier, Perth loves a good claim to fame. Even though the AC/DC frontman wasn't technically born here, he moved to Fremantle with his family in 1956 and his ashes are interred in Fremantle Cemetery. Fans of Bon Scott raised $45,000 to see this monument erected. This is exactly what it says on the tin, but absolutely worth a visit for the photo - especially if you are among the band's legions of fans. Enter the cemetery near the corner of High and Carrington Sts and you'll find Bon's plaque on the left about 15 metres inside.

33. HEAR THE CRASHING OF SERPENTINE FALLS

Definitely worth a visit if you are exploring some of the sights to the south of Perth. The Serpentine Falls is a beautiful place to spend an afternoon and is also a sanctuary for an array of plants and animals (particularly kangaroos). Picture this: the smell of gum leaves, the hiss of cicadas and the sun's setting rays piercing through the few wisps of cloud, while you're sitting with a cup of Fruity Lexia listening to the crashing of the waterfall into the pool below. Pure magic is seen and felt at Serpentine Falls.

34. GET A REVOLVING VIEW OF THE CITY

Nestled high among Perth's striking skyline is the C Restaurant - the city's only revolving restaurant.

Taking 90 minutes to do a full rotation, this is happening while diners get their forks into a three-course meal or the ever popular high tea. Find it on the 33rd floor of St Martins Tower on St Georges Terrace.

35. RUN AWAY AND JOIN THE CIRCUS

The WA Circus School (WACS) is a not-for-profit organization dedicated to promoting circus arts to curious adults and children alike. Having been around for more than 10 years, tucked away in the west end of Fremantle, you're likely to meet a variety of local performers using the venue as practice space and a social hub. Sign up for classes in everything from aerial performance and juggling to fire twirling and chair balancing.

36. WORK ON YOUR TAN AT COTTESLOE BEACH

The metro area of Perth has a string of 19 beautifully clean and uncrowded beaches and Cottesloe Beach is probably the most iconic. Cottesloe Beach is located midway between the Perth central business district and the port of Fremantle in Perth's western suburbs, only 15 minutes from the city. Besides the clear ocean water and white beaches, are grassed terraces and parks behind the beach with tall shady Norfolk Island pine trees to protect you from the heat of the day. It is one of the city's favorite beaches for families to go swimming, snorkelling, surfing or simply watching the beautiful sunsets over the Indian Ocean. Cottesloe Beach is also a favorite with wind surfers, sailboarders and kite fliers, so there is always something happening on the water or in the air. When you have finished up at the beach visit the art-deco Indiana Teahouse where you can enjoy a delicious meal at the restaurant upstairs while gazing over the ocean. Across the road from the beach you can also find a row of cafes, surf shops, pubs and restaurants bustling with activity.

37. GET LOST IN A BOOK AT THE STATE LIBRARY

The State Library of Western Australia is a research, reference and public lending library located in the Perth Cultural Centre in Perth City. The State Library of Western Australia is responsible for collecting and preserving Western Australia's documentary heritage. The J. S. Battye Library of Western Australian History is the arm of the library dedicated to Western Australian materials and contains a comprehensive collection of books published in Western Australia, books by a Western Australian or about Western Australia published elsewhere. It also contains a comprehensive coverage of West Australian newspapers, a more selective coverage of serials and maps published in Western Australia. The library also has extensive collections of original manuscripts, journals, diaries and letters of individuals, records of non-government organisations, Western Australian music recordings, Western Australian photographs and films, oral history recordings and transcripts. The library has a specialist family history section where volunteers from the Western Australian Genealogical Society provide assistance to clients. A dedicated children's area is also available for younger readers. The library holds over 50,000 music scores, potentially making it one of the largest public music lending libraries in Australia.

38. BRUSH UP ON YOUR HISTORY

The Western Australian Museum is Western Australia's premier cultural organization, housing WA's scientific and cultural collection.   It has three main sites around Perth: within the Perth Cultural Centre and two in Fremantle (the Maritime and Shipwreck Galleries). During 1959, the botanical collection was transferred to the new herbarium and the museum and the art gallery became separate institutions.   The museum has focused its collecting and research interests in the areas of natural sciences, anthropology, archaeology, and Western Australia's history. Through the 60s and 70s the museum began to work in historic shipwrecks and Aboriginal site management. The Western Australian Maritime Museum is located on Victoria Quay and contains galleries with themes, such as the Indian Ocean, the Swan River, fishing, maritime trade and naval defense. Nearby, on Cliff Street is the Western Australian Shipwreck Galleries Museum which is recognized as the foremost maritime archaeology and shipwreck conservation museum in the southern hemisphere. The museum is housed in an 1850s-era Commissariat building and contains a reconstructed hull from the Batavia, which was wrecked off the coast of Western Australia in 1629.

39. HEAR THE BELLS RING

The Swan Bells are a set of 18 bells hanging in a
82.5 m-high copper and glass campanile on the shore
of the Swan River in Perth City. The tower is
commonly known as The Bell Tower or the Swan
Bell Tower. The Swan Bells at the Bell Tower are
one of the largest musical instruments on Earth and
echoes throughout Perth City. Forming a sixteen-bell
peal with two extra chromatic notes, they are one of
the largest sets of change ringing bells in the world.
Twelve of the set are historic bells from St Martin-in-
the-Fields church in Trafalgar Square in London and
can be traced back to before the 14th century. They
are one of a few sets of royal bells and the only set
known to have left England. The St Martin-in-the-
Fields bells were donated to the State of Western

59

Australia as part of the 1988 Australian bicentenary celebration.

40. SPEND A DAY ON THE WATER

Hillarys Boat Harbour is a marina and tourist precinct north of Perth and is full of things to do. It is home to the elite Hillarys Yacht Club and AQWA (The Aquarium of Western Australia). The boat harbour features a busy retail shopping precinct (Sorrento Quay and Sorrento Quay Boardwalk) and is surrounded by public parklands with an ocean swimmers cove. Hillarys Boat Harbour is really popular with locals and overseas visitors alike. In fact, for many it is a weekly activity. Hillarys Boat Harbour thrives as the hub for various tourist activities like adventure fishing, coastal heli-tours, diving and whale-watching charters.

"It feels good to be lost in the right direction."

41. WALK AMONG THE TREETOPS

Get lost in nature with a walk along the Federation Walkway which continues to draw tourists and locals alike. The peaceful pathway has been carefully plotted to enable visitors to experience the range of flora and fauna available in Kings Park's Botanical Garden. The path stretches across 620 meters and includes a 222 m-long glass-and-steel bridge that passes through a canopy of eucalypts.

42. DRINK A CHAI CHILLER AT DOME CAFÉ

There are a few of these cafes dotted around Perth and surrounding areas, but the best is the one on the Mandurah Foreshore where you can watch dolphins play in the water right in front of you as you sip your coffee. Dome has become somewhat of an institution for Perthians who have moved away or overseas, usually acting as the meeting point for visits back home. The menu could be mistaken for your usual cafe fare, except the food is actually delicious. Top recommendations include the beef burger, the BLT, the chocolate cake and their delicious chai chillers.

43. HAVE A PICNIC AT WATERMAN'S BAY

One of the best places in Perth to watch the change of day is Waterman's Bay. Containing all the facilities you might need to camp out and watch the beautiful spectrum of colors reach across the Indian Ocean as the sun dips below the horizon. Take a picnic blanket and stretch out on the luscious green grass overlooked by a series of rocky cliff faces.

44. WATCH SOME RUBBER BURN

A little short of the F1, the Perth Motorplex can be equally as exciting. Whether a high-profile event or just your average group of drifters with too much money to burn, you will definitely get your blood pumping. Top events include drag racing, speedway, burnouts, Motorvation, and Whoop Ass Wednesday.

45. GO CAMPING

Pack the tent, a bag of snacks and head to Dwellingup, just south of Perth, for a wonderful camping experience any time of year. Lane Poole Reserve is the most popular with the Murray River providing raging rapids and waterfalls in the winter and a smooth stream for swimming or fishing in the summer. In the spring, the forest bursts with a colorful array of wildflowers and in the autumn it swells with birdsong courtesy of the parrots and magpies.

46. FEEL LIKE A GIANT

For something a little more quirky, head to Amaze Miniature Park, formerly known as Abingdon Miniature Village. Walk around the beautifully manicured gardens adorned with miniature buildings that replicate a tiny version of the original town of Abingdon in England. There is a mini golf course within the park if looking at tiny buildings is not enough to keep you occupied.

47. EAT REALLY GOOD GELATO

Perth is known for its scorching temperatures, which is why it has become home to some very good gelato. The best by far is Gusto Gelato, owned by Sean Lee, who studied his artisan techniques in Bologna, Italy. This handcrafted gelato is to die for and comes in a wide variety of flavors. Definitely try the salted caramel or the cheesecake to awaken your palette!

48. WATCH HOW CHOCOLATE IS MADE

If you have a sweet tooth, make the journey to Decadent Cs chocolate factory. They source all of their chocolate from Belgium before processing it in-house into all manner of delicious things, like truffles and chocolate-covered pretzels. Sample some of these goodies in the café before watching the magic unfold from the factory room viewing window at the front of the shop.

49. FLY THROUGH THE AIR

For the young or young at heart, head to Cannington's all-age trampoline park, BounceInc, for an adrenaline-filled afternoon. One part of the venue is filled with trampolines, allowing you to bounce off the walls to your heart's delight, while the other half is dedicated to the X-Park adventure challenge course. Similar to American Ninja Warrior, this obstacle course requires you to get from the start to the end in the fastest and most awesome way possible.

50. FINISH YOUR DAY OFF WITH A COCKTAIL

Inspired by the era of pre-prohibition and the speakeasy, Alter Ego has the most impressive list of cocktails created. Housed inside The Mantle, this relaxed bar is the perfect place to unwind after a busy day of sightseeing. My top recommendation goes to the rum-rich Steel Embrace espresso martini, but check their Facebook page for their latest craft cocktail creations!

TOP REASONS TO BOOK THIS TRIP

- **Sun sets**: The sun sets in the West, which means you can watch the sun sink below the horizon while being reflected from one of Perth's many beautiful beaches.

- **Culture**: Perth's isolation from other cities means it has developed a rich culture, uninfluenced by other parts of Australia.

- **Food**: Perth has developed a rich foodie culture, with unique restaurants and eating experiences dotted across the city.

PACKING AND PLANNING TIPS

A Week before Leaving

- Arrange for someone to take care of pets and water plants.

- Email and Print important Documents.

- Get Visa and vaccines if needed.

- Check for travel warnings.

- Stop mail and newspaper.

- Notify Credit Card companies where you are going.

- Passports and photo identification is up to date.

- Pay bills.

- Copy important items and download travel Apps.

- Start collecting small bills for tips.

- Have post office hold mail while you are away.

- Check weather for the week.

- Car inspected, oil is changed, and tires have the correct pressure.

- Check airline luggage restrictions.

- Download Apps needed for your trip.

Right Before Leaving

- Contact bank and credit cards to tell them your location.

- Clean out refrigerator.

- Empty garbage cans.

- Lock windows.

- Make sure you have the proper identification with you.

- Bring cash for tips.

- Remember travel documents.

- Lock door behind you.

- Remember wallet.

- Unplug items in house and pack chargers.

- Change your thermostat settings.

- Charge electronics, and prepare camera memory cards.

READ OTHER
GREATER THAN A TOURIST
BOOKS

Greater Than a Tourist- Geneva Switzerland: 50 Travel Tips from a Local by Amalia Kartika

Greater Than a Tourist- St. Croix US Birgin Islands USA: 50 Travel Tips from a Local by Tracy Birdsall

Greater Than a Tourist- San Juan Puerto Rico: 50 Travel Tips from a Local by Melissa Tait

Greater Than a Tourist – Lake George Area New York USA: 50 Travel Tips from a Local by Janine Hirschklau

Greater Than a Tourist – Monterey California United States: 50 Travel Tips from a Local by Katie Begley

Greater Than a Tourist – Chanai Crete Greece: 50 Travel Tips from a Local by Dimitra Papagrigoraki

Greater Than a Tourist – The Garden Route Western Cape Province South Africa: 50 Travel Tips from a Local by Li-Anne McGregor van Aardt

Greater Than a Tourist – Sevilla Andalusia Spain: 50 Travel Tips from a Local by Gabi Gazon

Children's Book: *Charlie the Cavalier Travels the World* by Lisa Rusczyk

73

> TOURIST

Visit *Greater Than a Tourist* for Free Travel Tips
http://GreaterThanATourist.com

Sign up for the *Greater Than a Tourist* Newsletter for
discount days, new books, and travel information:
http://eepurl.com/cxspyf

Follow us on Facebook for tips, images, and ideas:
https://www.facebook.com/GreaterThanATourist

Follow us on Pinterest for travel tips and ideas:
http://pinterest.com/GreaterThanATourist

Follow us on Instagram for beautiful travel images:
http://Instagram.com/GreaterThanATourist

Follow *Greater Than a Tourist* on Amazon.

At *Greater Than a Tourist*, we love to share travel tips with you. How did we do? What guidance do you have for how we can give you better advice for your next trip? Please send your feedback to GreaterThanaTourist@gmail.com as we continue to improve the series. We appreciate your constructive feedback. Thank you.

METRIC CONVERSIONS

TEMPERATURE

```
110° F —          — 40° C
100° F —
 90° F —          — 30° C
 80° F —
 70° F —          — 20° C
 60° F —
 50° F —          — 10° C
 40° F —
 32° F —          — 0° C
 20° F —
 10° F —          — -10° C
  0° F —          — -18° C
-10° F —
-20° F —          — -30° C
```

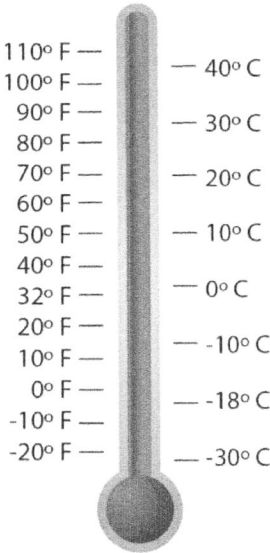

To convert F to C:

Subtract 32, and then multiply by 5/9 or .5555.

To Convert C to F:

Multiply by 1.8 and then add 32.

32F = 0C

LIQUID VOLUME

To Convert:...................Multiply by
U.S. Gallons to Liters................ 3.8
U.S. Liters to Gallons 26
Imperial Gallons to U.S. Gallons 1.2
Imperial Gallons to Liters....... 4.55
Liters to Imperial Gallons 22
1 Liter = .26 U.S. Gallon
1 U.S. Gallon = 3.8 Liters

DISTANCE

To convert ....Multiply by
Inches to Centimeters 2.54
Centimeters to Inches 39
Feet to Meters...................... .3
Meters to Feet 3.28
Yards to Meters 91
Meters to Yards 1.09
Miles to Kilometers 1.61
Kilometers to Miles............ .62
1 Mile = 1.6 km
1 km = .62 Miles

WEIGHT

1 Ounce = .28 Grams
1 Pound = .4555 Kilograms
1 Gram = .04 Ounce
1 Kilogram = 2.2 Pounds

TRAVEL QUESTIONS

- Do you bring presents home to family or friends after a vacation?

- Do you get motion sick?

- Do you have a favorite billboard?

- Do you know what to do if there is a flat tire?

- Do you like a sun roof open?

- Do you like to eat in the car?

- Do you like to wear sun glasses in the car?

- Do you like toppings on your ice cream?

- Do you use public bathrooms?

- Did you bring your cell phone and does it have power?

- Do you have a form of identification with you?

- Have you ever been pulled over by a cop?

- Have you ever given money to a stranger on a road trip?

- Have you ever taken a road trip with animals?

- Have you ever went on a vacation alone?

- Have you ever run out of gas?

- If you could move to any place in the world, where would it be?

- If you could travel anywhere in the world, where would you travel?

- If you could travel in any vehicle, which one would it be?

- If you had three things to wish for from a magic genie, what would they be?

- If you have a driver's license, how many times did it take you to pass the test?

- What are you the most afraid of on vacation?

- What do you want to get away from the most when you are on vacation?

- What foods smells bad to you?

- What item do you bring on ever trip with you away from home?

- What makes you sleepy?

- What song would you love to hear on the radio when you're cruising on the highway?

- What travel job would you want the least?

- What will you miss most while you are away from home?

- What is something you always wanted to try?

- What is the best road side attraction that you ever saw?

- What is the farthest distance you ever biked?

- What is the farthest distance you ever walked?

- What is the weirdest thing you needed to buy while on vacation?

- What is your favorite candy?

- What is your favorite color car?

- What is your favorite family vacation?

- What is your favorite food?

- What is your favorite gas station drink or food?

- What is your favorite license plate design?

- What is your favorite restaurant?

- What is your favorite smell?

- What is your favorite song?

- What is your favorite sound that nature makes?

- What is your favorite thing to bring home from a vacation?

- What is your favorite vacation with friends?

- What is your favorite way to relax?

- Where is the farthest place you ever traveled in a car?

- Where is the farthest place you ever went North, South, East and West?

- Where is your favorite place in the world?

- Who is your favorite singer?

- Who taught you how to drive?

- Who will you miss the most while you are away?

- Who if the first person you will contact when you get to your destination?

- Who brought you on your first vacation?

- Who likes to travel the most in your life?

- Would you rather be hot or cold?

- Would you rather drive above, below, or at the speed limited?

- Would you rather drive on a highway or a back road?

- Would you rather go on a train or a boat?

- Would you rather go to the beach or the woods?

>TOURIST

TRAVEL BUCKET LIST

1.

2.

3.

4.

5.

6.

7.

8.

9.

10.

>TOURIST

Printed in Great Britain
by Amazon